Words that are in bold, like **this**, are explained in the Word help, on the page and at the end of the book.

The *Made in South Africa* series is published by
Awareness Publishing Group (Pty) Ltd.
Copyright © 2019

Awareness Publishing (SA) (Pty) Ltd
www.awareness.co.za
info@awareness.co.za
+27 (0)86 110 1491
www.facebook.com/AwarenessPublishing

All rights reserved. No part of this publication may be reproduced in any form without written permission from the publisher, except by a reviewer.

First edition 2019

The story of rooibos tea by Lynn Barnes
ISBN 978-1-77008-989-1

Summary: A simple introduction to rooibos tea, including some details of its history in South Africa, how it grows and how it is made.

Book design: Richard Keenan-Smith and Elizabeth Barnard

Editorial credits: Managing editor: Monique le Riché; Copy editor: Danya Ristić-Schacherl; Picture editors: Anne Laing and Lawrence Frank

Picture credits: Cover © Anne Laing; cover (background) © Rooibos Limited; cover (flag) © Kurt / Dreamstime; endpapers © wisan224 / iStock; p4 © Anne Laing; p6 © Rooibos Limited; p8 © Rooibos Limited; p10 © René Hermans; p11 © Rooibos Limited; p12 © Rooibos Limited; p14 © Anne Laing; p16 © WJ Huggins / Wikipedia; p18 © Tick Tock Teas; p18 (inset) © Rooibos Limited; p20 © Dr FJ Strauss; p22 © Rooibos Limited; p23 © Old Mutual Foundation road trip; p24 © Cobus Prinsloo; p26 © Rooibos Limited; p28 © Jeremy Glyn; p30 © Andrey_Kuzmin / Shutterstock; p32 (all) © Rooibos Limited; p34 © Anne Laing; p36 © Anne Laing; p38 © Anne Laing; p40 © Rooibos Limited

1 3 5 7 9 0 8 6 4 2

Contents

Rooibos tea 5
Red tea from a green bush 7
Only in South Africa 9
The first people to make rooibos tea 11
Collecting the branches and leaves 13
A refreshing drink 15
Settlers from Europe 17
Benjamin Ginsberg 19
Growing the bushes 21
Getting the seeds 23
Ants like rooibos too 25
Rooibos farms 27
Rooibos tea for health 29
Treating illnesses 31
From the fields to the factory 33
Making rooibos tea 35
Drinking rooibos tea 37
Word help 39

Many South Africans love rooibos tea.

Rooibos tea

People in South Africa have been drinking rooibos tea for hundreds of years. They like the taste of it and also believe it is good for their health.

Rooibos bushes growing in the Cederberg area of South Africa.

Red tea from a green bush

Rooibos tea is red, and is made from the branches and leaves of a bush.

The leaves are green when they are growing on the bush, but they turn red when they are dried to make the tea.

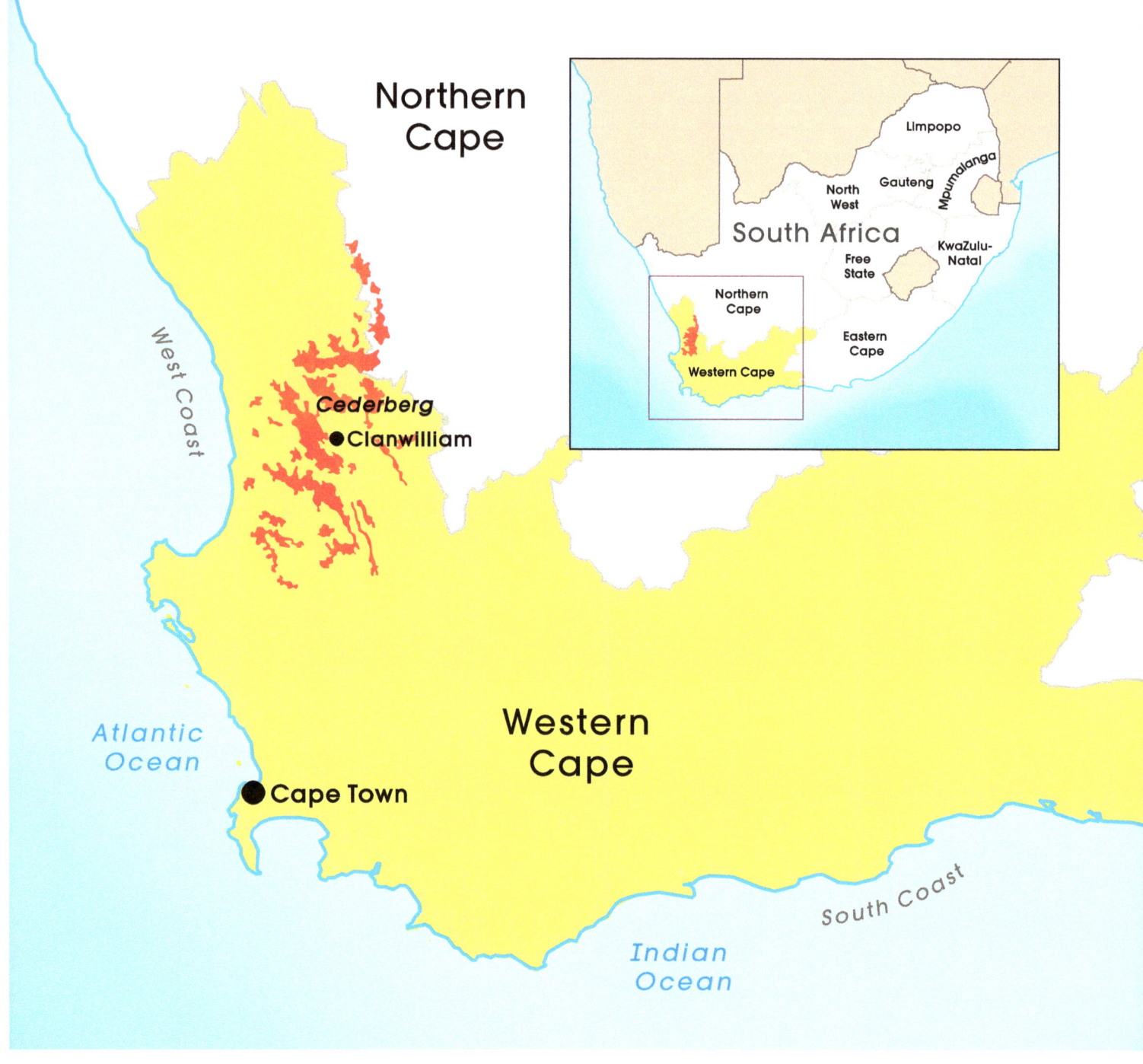

The red area shows where rooibos bushes grow.

Only in South Africa

The rooibos bush grows only in one small area called Cederberg. This is a mountainous area near the coast in Western Cape province in South Africa.

People in other countries, such as China, Australia and the United States of America, have tried to grow the bush, but they have never been able to do it.

Cederberg, where rooibos bushes grow naturally.

The first people to make rooibos tea

Over 300 years ago, the people living in the Cederberg area saw the rooibos bushes growing there. They discovered that they could use the very thin branches and soft, needle-like leaves of the bush to make a refreshing drink, and also to make medicines.

The very thin branches and needle-like leaves of the rooibos bush.

A man carrying bundles of branches and leaves that have been cut from the rooibos bushes.

Collecting the branches and leaves

The people living in the Cederberg area climbed the sides of the mountains to find the rooibos bushes, which were growing wild. They cut off the thin branches and leaves, fastened them together in bundles, and carried them down the mountains.

Rooibos branches and leaves that have been chopped into small pieces and dried.

A refreshing drink

The people chopped the branches and leaves into pieces and hit them with hammers to crush them. Then they left them in the sun to dry. The dried pieces would then keep for a long time.

People made a kind of tea by soaking the dried pieces in boiling water.

Ships like this brought tea from Europe to South Africa.

Settlers from Europe

In 1652 people started to come from Europe to settle in South Africa. These people liked to drink a kind of tea called black tea. But bringing this tea in ships all the way from Europe took a long time and was very expensive. So they started drinking the local rooibos tea instead.

The Ginsberg family's "Eleven-O'clock" rooibos tea brand.
Inset: **Benjamin Ginsberg.**

Benjamin Ginsberg

Benjamin Ginsberg was a Jewish man who came from Russia to settle in South Africa. In 1904, he became interested in the tea made from bushes that grew wild in the mountains. He did many experiments at Rondegat Farm to find the best way to **treat** the leaves for making tea.

Benjamin Ginsberg was the first person to start selling rooibos tea to other countries in the world.

> **Word help**
>
> **treat:** when you treat something you do something to it, such as wash it, heat it, crush it or dry it

Dr Le Fras Nortier first started growing rooibos bushes on Klein Kliphuis Farm near Clanwilliam in the 1930s.

Growing the bushes

It was not easy to get the branches and leaves from the wild rooibos bushes in the mountains. So in the 1930s Ginsberg asked a local doctor, Le Fras Nortier, to try to grow the rooibos bushes on a farm called Klein Kliphuis.

Each flower on the rooibos bush contains one tiny seed.

Getting the seeds

To grow rooibos bushes, Dr Nortier needed seeds. But rooibos seeds are very small and they easily blow away in the wind. He struggled to collect seeds for his rooibos farm, so he bought rooibos seeds from anyone who could find them in the Cederberg mountains.

Rooibos seeds.

A picture showing what an ants' nest looks like underground.

Ants like rooibos too

One woman found an **unusual** way to collect the seeds. One day, she saw some ants carrying seeds and she followed the ants back to their nest. When she broke open the nest, it was full of rooibos seeds. It was easier to take seeds from ants' nests than to find the seeds herself!

> **Word help**
> **unusual:** not usual; different or strange

Today there are many rooibos farms in the area around Clanwilliam in the Cederberg.

Rooibos farms

Dr Nortier managed to grow the rooibos bushes, and Klein Kliphuis became a tea farm. As more people started to drink rooibos tea, the price of rooibos seeds went up. In the 1940s rooibos was the most expensive vegetable seed in the world!

Nowadays, the seeds are collected from the ground underneath the bushes.

Rooibos tea is safe for anyone to drink at any time. Unlike most other types of tea, rooibos tea contains no caffeine.

Rooibos tea for health

Many people believe that rooibos tea is good for their health. It is a **natural** product with nothing added to give it colour or make it last longer. And, unlike most other teas, it does not contain **caffeine**, which is not good for the body.

> **Word help**
>
> **natural:** coming from nature, not made by people
>
> **caffeine:** a type of drug that affects the brain and the body, making you feel more awake

Rooibos is safe for babies to drink.

Treating illnesses

Rooibos tea contains many things that are good for the body. People say that it can help with headaches, stomach pains, skin problems and even **cancer**. It is also safe enough to give to babies to help them sleep.

> **Word help**
> **cancer:** a very serious disease

1

2

3

4

From the fields to the factory

Today, rooibos tea is still produced in much the same way as the people in the Cederberg did it long ago. The branches and leaves of the bush are cut into very small pieces, crushed and then spread out to dry. But it is made in larger quantities in a factory, using modern machines.

1. Workers use a sharp tool to cut the growing rooibos bushes.
2. People working at the factory where machines clean the branches and leaves, cut them into small pieces and crush them.
3. Tractors spread the small pieces out to dry in the sun.
4. When the pieces are dry they are put into sacks and sent to companies that sell tea.

Many different kinds of rooibos tea are sold in shops.

Making rooibos tea

We can buy rooibos tea in shops and supermarkets.

Many companies sell the small dried pieces in boxes or as tea bags.

To make a drink, the tea needs to be added to boiling water and then left for a few minutes so that the **flavour** grows stronger.

> **Word help**
> **flavour:** taste

Some people add sugar or honey to rooibos tea to sweeten it.

Drinking rooibos tea

We can drink rooibos tea hot or cold, and with or without milk and sugar. Many people like to drink it hot with a slice of lemon and some honey to sweeten it. Other people make the tea and then add ice to it.

Do you have a favourite way to drink rooibos tea?

You can even make ice cream flavoured with rooibos tea!

Word help

caffeine: a type of drug that affects the brain and the body, making you feel more awake

cancer: a very serious disease

flavour: taste

natural: coming from nature, not made by people

treat: when you treat something you do something to it, such as wash it, heat it, crush it or dry it

unusual: not usual; different or strange

A rooibos tea box from about 1915.

www.ingramcontent.com/pod-product-compliance
Lightning Source LLC
Chambersburg PA
CBHW051259110526
44589CB00025B/2883